Kid Creations

by Robynne Eagan

illustrated by Darcy Tom

Teaching & Learning Company

1204 Buchanan St., P.O. Box 10
Carthage, IL 62321

The activities shown on the front cover are
Homemade Chalk (page 14) and the Homemade Chalkboard (page 7).

Cover photo by Girard Photography

Copyright © 1994, Teaching & Learning Company

ISBN No. 1-57310-009-9

Printing No. 98765432

Teaching & Learning Company
1204 Buchanan St., P.O. Box 10
Carthage, IL 62321

This book belongs to

_____

Acknowledgements

I would like to thank the many children who have made this book possible through their yearning to explore and create–especially Kiersten, Ben and Bailey who can make anything out of anything. Thanks to Charlie for his ideas, to Al and Sandy Cochrane (my parents) for their artistic influence, to Tracey Schofield for her editing and to Carol Goulette for sharing her creativity.

I am grateful to all of the inventive individuals who directly or inadvertently have contributed to this compilation for the past 16 years. Your recipes are continuing to excite children!

I would also like to thank all of the creative educators, parents, outdoor recreation leaders and summer camp staffs for their experimentation, keen interest and ability to pass their enthusiasm on to children.

Table of Contents

Chapter 1: Things to Create On 5

Chapter 2: Things to Paint and Draw With . . .12

Foreword

Kid Creations is a lively collection of recipes for art supplies and creative suggestions for implementing these in the primary classroom. This book is designed to generate fun, skill-based experiences in the primary art program. Children will have the opportunity to explore, express themselves freely and experience the pure joy of creating.

Dear Teacher or Parent,

Care to transform your room into a studio for creative learning?

Kid Creations turns creative stirrings into art supplies and works of art. This lively collection offers a refreshing approach to a skill-based classroom art program that begins with the making of basic materials. The making and use of these kid-doable, affordable, environmentally friendly recipes for art supplies integrates into all areas of the primary curriculum and sets the stage for stimulating artistic exploration.

Making and creating is essential to the development of children in kindergarten to grade 3, when their senses are rapidly developing and they are mastering a multitude of new skills. This book introduces children to a complete range of art materials and color media. Making their own materials using age-old methods gives children a sense of empowerment and control and manipulating these materials allows children to learn through their own senses. From pouring and stirring to feeling and forming, art media allows children to discover and develop in a manner that complements their natural ability to learn.

As a resource tool, *Kid Creations* offers educators a palette of ways to expand the child's world and add sparkle to the learning environment. The book is divided into sections based on artistic media. Recipes are presented in a clear, step-by-step manner with symbols for at-a-glance information (see page 1). Aims, objectives, skill development goals, curriculum links, extension activities, resources and a progress assessment chart are provided. Educators can enhance or simplify all activities to target particular developmental levels.

Educators (and children) who like to shake, mix, brew, rattle and roll—and get their hands dirty—can turn common ingredients into works of art and an art program into a hands-on adventure. With a little help from nature's treasure chest and the kitchen cupboard, these easy-to-follow recipes will enable children to achieve their full creative potential.

Roll up your sleeves, choose a recipe and stir up some creativity!

Sincerely,

Robynne

Robynne Eagan

Symbol Key

These symbols will provide at-a-glance information regarding the preparation of the mixtures.

 K, 1, 2, 3   Recommended grade level

 Full child participation in preparation

 Partial child participation in preparation

 Caution, extra supervision advised

 Ten minutes of active preparation time

 Ten to sixty minutes of active preparation time

 Over one hour of active preparation time

 Good group project

 Edible

 Ingredients may be hard to find

 Gift

 Large space requirements

 Mixture needs cooking

 Material will last for one to two weeks

 Material will last for one to two months

 Material will last for over three months

Messy

Skill Development

• •

Art media offers rich opportunity for the development of many skills. The materials and activities suggested in this book can be used as needed to facilitate the development of various skills. Refer to these words to see which skills are targeted by a particular activity.

Intellectual

Social

Emotional

Physical Development (fine and gross motor)

Language

Curriculum Links

• •

Each of the activities can be extended and incorporated into the study of a wider topic, and cross into various curriculum areas. Within the curriculum areas listed below, the materials and projects can be used to help develop any number of concepts. These words are used to indicate which curriculum area an activity most easily fits into.

Language	History
Math	Physical Education
Art	Health
Science	Music
Geography	

Measurement Equivalents

These will be useful if you divide recipes into small units to enable greater participation.

1 tablespoon = 3 teaspoons
1/2 tablespoon = 1 1/2 teaspoons
4 tablespoons = 1/4 cup
5 tablespoons and 1 teaspoon = 1/3 cup

Metric Conversions:

1 dry ounce = 28 grams
1 dry pound = 373 grams
1 liquid ounce = 29.5 milliliters
1 cup = .24 liter
1 pint = .47 liter
1 quart = .95 liter
1 gallon = 3.8 liters

1 cup = 250 milliliters
1/2 cup = 125 milliliters
1 teaspoon = 5 milliliters
1 tablespoon = 15 milliliters
1/4 cup = 60 milliliters
1 inch = 2.54 centimeters
1/4-inch thickness = 5 millimeters thickness

Oven Temperatures:

230°F = 110°C
275°F = 135°C
325°F = 163°C
350°F = 177°C
375°F = 191°C
400°F = 204°C

Guidelines to Facilitate Creative Learning

1. Respect a child's right to create.
   Allow children to explore with materials and express their *own* ideas.
   Introduce skills, techniques and tools in response to a child's curiosity and needs.
   Once students have had the opportunity for free exploration of materials, then tools, props, suggestions, models and samples can be provided to further develop and introduce particular skills.

2. Organize in advance. Read instructions, have materials ready to go and make a sample in a trial run of the activity. Kids should be able to explore and create with little or no educator assistance.

3. Provide ample creative space and materials for natural artistic exploration.

4. Have flexible expectations and expect unpredictable results.

5. Show appreciation of children's exploration by recognizing their efforts as artistic accomplishments. Show interest, give positive comments and let the child volunteer information.

6. Evaluate the child's growth through observation of a wide variety of artistic experiences. Focus on the process of creating, not the end product.

7. Expect things to get messy! Allow for creative problem solving and choices when you incorporate cleanup into the activity.

8. Provide a means to show or keep works as students will emotionally bond to these creations.

Chapter 1

Things to Create On
The Clean Slate

Surfaces to explore scribbles, lines and shapes are very important. Each child has unique responses to different surfaces. A sense of ownership comes with a self-made means and surfaces for creating and work on these becomes more meaningful.

Aims:
- To involve the child in the making of practical work surfaces.
- To encourage problem solving through the construction of various practical work surfaces.
- To encourage the development of group skills.
- To promote self-esteem in the child.

Objectives:
- Child will make various surfaces for later artistic activities.
- Child will develop fine and large motor skills through the making of these items.
- Child will experience a sense of self-work through making of these surfaces.

Skill Development:
- Intellectual
- Emotional
- Gross Motor
- Social
- Fine Motor
- Language

Curriculum Links:
- Language
- Science
- History
- Math
- Art

Homemade Felt Board

 2-3

This item can be used over and over again for various projects and activities.

Materials:

heavy cardboard or light wood panel board
felt piece, larger than the board
small felt bits in bright and contrasting colors
scissors
electric tape

Process:

1. Cover the board with felt. Wrap the felt around so that it is smooth on the front surface. Helping hands can keep the felt taut as it is pulled around to the back of the board.
2. Tape the felt on the back side of the board.
3. Cut various sized shapes, letters, characters and numbers from felt pieces.

Try This:

- Choose a theme and go wild with felt. Kids can create their own theme-oriented pieces. Teachers and students can use the board to talk about themes and concepts.
- Kids and educators can create felt puzzles to be pieced together on the board.
- Teachers and students can use the board as a wonderful medium for story-telling.
- Adhere fun shapes to boards individually, in small groups or as one large group.
- Use the board as a daily calendar in conjunction with a math program.

Homemade Chalkboard

 K-3

Materials:

chalkboard paint (spray paint or tin from hobby or hardware stores)
heavy cardboard or masonite board
paintbrush
edging tape (masking, cloth or electric)
old sock
chalk

Process:

1. In a well-ventilated area, brush or spray chalkboard paint on the board. Let it dry completely.
2. Trim the edges of the board with tape.
3. The child's very own chalkboard is ready to use! See chalk recipe on page 14. The old sock that lost its mate can be used to erase.

Try This:

- Make one large board or individual chalkboards for each child.
- Challenge students to measure and tape their boards as neatly as possible.
- Children can individualize their boards with acrylic paint borders or logos.
- Incorporate measurement concepts in this activity.
- Provide colored chalk, tracers and alphabet cards.
- Use the boards for math lessons, to record bird-watching results, to keep tallies and to make pictures.
- Explore chalking techniques. Chalk on a damp board, use pointy chalk, the edge and the side of the chalk. How many different lines can you make?

* Caution: Paint in open air!

Recycled Paper

1-3   🧍   over 1 hour   🙌   🎁   SPACE

Materials:

newspapers
bucket
water
wire whisk
3 T (15 ml) cornstarch
1 cup (250 ml) water
measuring spoons
piece of screen or wire mesh
    about 6" (15.24 cm) across
plastic wrap to cover screen

Process:

1. Tear newspapers into very small pieces and drop them in a bucket. (Students like to do this!)
2. When the bucket is half-full of newspaper pieces, add enough water to wet all of the pieces.
3. Let the soggy mess stand for at least two hours.
4. Beat the mess to a creamy pulp using the whisk.
5. Dissolve cornstarch in 1 cup (250 ml) of water and mix in with the pulp.
6. Spread sheets of newspaper on a work surface large enough to lay the screen on.
7. Submerge the piece of screen into the mixture and gently lift it out. Repeat this several times until the screen has about 1/8" (.3 cm) of pulp on it.
8. Lay the pulp-covered screen on top of the newspaper-covered surface.
9. Cover the pulpy screen with plastic wrap.
10. Remove excess water from the screen by blotting over plastic with a towel. Children can take turns with this task.
11. Set the screen up so air can dry the pulp.
12. When dry, gently peel your recycled paper from screen.

TLC10009 Copyright © Teaching & Learning Company, Carthage, IL 62321

Recycled Paper

Try This:

- Use your recycled paper as a decorative paper for a special project.
- Make paper kites that fly with string or a simple kite that flies from a thin stick.
- Experiment with a large window screen to make a large piece of paper.
- Mix a batch of paper in the blender reducing recipe to fit the appliance.
- Pour the mixture into a clay mold. Remove when dry to create a raised form that can be painted and/or framed.
- Incorporate counting as students drop newspaper pieces into the bucket, one at a time, two at a time and so on. Estimate how many pieces it will take to half fill the bucket.
- Explore $1/2$" (1.25 cm), $1/8$" (.3 cm) and 1" (2.54 cm). What else in your room is $1/8$" (.3 cm) thick?
- How does the pulp turn into paper? Introduce the concept of evaporation.
  - How long is two hours? Turn paper making into a lesson on telling time . . . while you wait for the messy mixture to be ready for stirring.

Anything Paper

1-3

Materials:

lint (from clothes dryer)
cake pan
rags
choice of flowers, grass, weeds,
    leaves, paper towels,
    colored paper, newspaper
water
wire mesh or old screen (to fit pan)
heavy scissors

Process:

1. Cut wire mesh or old screen into a circle that fits easily inside a cake pan.
2. Place lint and gathered materials into cake pan.
3. Fill the pan with warm water to soak contents of pan and let stand for 5 minutes.
4. Prepare a rag-covered surface.
5. Submerge the screen into the mixture and lift out so that a layer of linty mush remains on top of the screen. Submerge again if you see any holes.
6. Blot the pulp very carefully with the rags.
7. Place the screen on a rag-covered surface to dry.

Try This:

- To the lint mixture, add very tiny bits of colored thread, dried grass, flowers, fabric pieces, weeds, etc. Encourage every student to contribute something. Admire and discuss the colors.
- Place lace, pressed flowers or leaves on the wet paper. These will dry into the paper.
- Add berries or other dye sources (see page 13) to the mixture for hued papers.
- Glue dried paper to used paper or construction paper and mat or frame.
- Ask children how the lint turned into paper. Introduce the concept of evaporation.
- Incorporate a lesson on time; have children time the five-minute waiting period.
- Challenge children to think about different kinds of paper. Children can suggest their own paper recipes.
- Incorporate a history lesson on the origins of paper. What did early peoples use?

Grinding Stone

K-3

A treasured tool that becomes an important work surface. The more it is used, the better it gets.

Materials:
large flat stone
hard stone able to fit in hand easily

Process:
1. Grind objects between the large and small stones. In time, a depression will form that will make the grinding of various ingredients much easier.
2. Use this tool as needed to create ingredients needed for various recipes.

Try This:
- Try grinding grains.
- Discuss early methods of making paints, foods and medicines. Compare these to current methods.

Chapter 2
Things to Paint and Draw With

Vibrant colors, neat textures and lines of all sorts make works of art. A class can make what they need to form lines by raiding the kitchen cupboard and finding a few other things around school or home. Students will scribble, shade and make lines and shapes with homemade chalk, crayons that are hard to resist and paint kids can't wait to get a brush into!

The predictable stages of drawing; Experimentation and Scribble, Pre-Schematic, Schematic and Representational Stages will progress naturally as children are presented with intriguing opportunities to make lines with all sorts of tools. Whether a child attempts to produce a representation of an object or merely enjoys the process, painting and drawing will encourage thoughtful observation, develop fine motor skills and reinforce a positive self-concept.

Aims:

- To involve the child in varied drawing, coloring and painting activities.
- To encourage children to explore drawing, coloring and painting techniques.
- To investigate art media in a wide variety of conditions.

Objectives:

- Child will explore properties of various media.
- Child will explore and experiment with a variety of painting and drawing.
- Child will develop graduated skills through use of various media.
- Child will develop skill in the handling and care of particular tools.

Skill Development:

- Intellectual
- Social
- Emotional
- Fine Motor
- Large Motor
- Language

Curriculum Links:

- Language
- Math
- Science
- Art
- Geography
- History
- Physical Education
- Music

12

Natural Pigment

K-3

Make the powdered colors needed to give your paints colors.

● ●

Materials:

grinding stone
smooth unbreakable surface (cutting board, Plexiglas™, paper plate)
natural pigment sources: berries, mud, clay, dirt, soft stones, sand, plants
synthetic pigment sources: drink crystals, colored chalks

● ●

Process:

1. Search for and gather the things you need to make interesting colors.
2. Put the pigment source on the surface and grind with your rock.

● ●

Try This:

• Natural pigments, tempera, watercolor paints, water crayons or food coloring can be used to color paints.
• Set up a Color Center where children can make pigment, add it to various media and create.

Homemade Chalk

K-3

Chalk is an excellent medium to create various textures, effects, colors and shades on all kinds of surfaces. Easy to make, stores well and cleans up in a flash.

Materials:

1 part water
2 parts plaster of Paris
small paper roll, rubber bands and wrap or paper cups

powdered tempera paint
spoon
mixing container
cloth or face mask

Process:

1. If using paper rolls, cover bottom of roll with wrap and hold in place with rubber band.
2. Mix tempera in water until darker than desired shade is reached.
3. Pour colored water into mixing container.
4. Gently pour plaster on top of water, and let sit until the plaster settles to the bottom.
5. Stir mixture with spoon or hands until it forms a creamy mixture.
6. Pour into small paper cups or paper roll forms.
7. Let the mixture dry until hard–at least one hour.
8. Peel off the paper form (If the chalk is damp, you may need to rub the chalk to remove paper residue.) and start chalkin'!

Try This:

- Decorate the school yard–it will wash away with the rain!
- Teach a unit on the old favorite chalk games of the school yard.
- Incorporate a study of historical children's games around the world.
- Incorporate a lesson in time as you wait one hour for the mixture to harden.
- Experiment with color.
- Make texture rubbings using chalk.
- Have students trace one another's silhouettes onto the school yard.
- Make a picture using chalk. Paint over it with water for a marbled effect.
- Variation: Use ground eggshells in place of plaster of Paris. Grind eggshells with a grinding stone until fine. This chalk will work best on the sidewalk.
- Ask students to think about who uses chalk and why? Consider teachers, sign writers, ballerinas, gymnasts, tailors and dressmakers and many more.
- Ask students to think about uses of chalk. Did they know it is found in various artistic mediums, cement, toothpaste, makeup and fertilizer? Real chalk consists of the remains of microscopic sea creatures from the Cretaceous period. In ancient Rome chalk was called "creta."

* Caution: Do not ingest plaster dust; keep dust down!

Charcoal

2-3

....

Materials:

charred wood
pocket knife or small saw
flat stone

....

Process:

1. All you have to do is find charred wood in the remains of a camp fire, fireplace or other place where wood has burned. You might find this opportunity on a field trip or nearby. You can even cheat and bring some charred wood to the classroom. Let kids break off chunks or cut pieces in a uniform manner with your pocket knife or small saw.
2. Rub the end of the charcoal stick on the stone to sharpen to a point.
3. Remember not to wear best whites for this activity and wash up after the picture making.

....

Try This:

- Charcoal works wonderfully on the homemade papers in this book or other thick papers.
- Use charcoal and thin paper to do rubbings of tree bark, brick walls and other interesting textures.
- Have students do five-minute charcoal sketches of "a model" in various poses.
- Talk about where charcoal comes from–part of a unit on trees perhaps.
- Study artwork completed by the masters in charcoal.
- Encourage kids to look around for subjects to sketch anytime, anyplace.

* Caution: Use caution when carving with pocket knife or saw.

Earth Colors

Materials:

2 ounces (56 g) beeswax
2 ounces (56 g) paraffin
5 tsp (25 ml) linseed oil
5 tsp (25 ml) natural pigment
old pan

spoon
old cupcake pan
foil cupcake cups
stove

Process:

1. Line the cupcake pan with foil cupcake cups.
2. Break up waxes and heat in pan over low heat until melted.
3. Remove from heat and slowly add oil and dry earth pigment to warm wax.
4. Stir until well mixed.
5. Pour warm mixture into cupcake cups and let cool.
6. Allow children to remove wax forms and have fun with earthy colors.

Try This:

- Allow students to choose earth pigments.
- Pour into paper rolls or other shapes to mold your crayons.
- Experiment with various waxes.
- Create a crayoned mural.
- An old paintbrush dipped in the almost-cool wax creates a neat effect on paper.
- Observe the progression in picture making from scribble to patches, to ovals, lines, dots, polliwogs and emerging head with significant features.
- Enhance a study of insects and bees.
- Embark on an investigation of crayons. How are they made? What colors are they?
- Talk about melting. What else melts? Observe ice cubes, gelatin and chocolate.

Egg Crayons

1-3

Materials:
crayon stubs
empty eggshells
tin can
egg carton
stove

Process:

1. Adult helpers can make the egg blowing go much easier! Use a large pointy needle to break a large hole in the narrow end of an egg.
2. Shake the egg until all of the contents are out. Rinse the inside and leave the eggshell to dry in egg carton.
3. Peel wrappers from crayons and drop the stubs into the can.
4. Put the can in pan of hot water and melt stubs until squishy with a few chunks floating.
5. Pour chunky wax into eggshells in egg carton. Fill each egg to the top.
6. Let the wax cool and harden (place in freezer for quick hardening).
7. Peel away eggshell to find a wax egg that really colors.

Try This:

- Give as a gift (great in spring).
- Mix colors for a rainbow effect.
- If time and resources are limited, break eggshells in half and set in carton.
- Melt crayon stubs in muffin tins in oven on low for some rainbow muffin crayons.
- Try "Alpha-Doodles"–turn letters into doodley characters.
- Cover an entire page with crayon color. Next, cover it all with black crayon, and then scratch off the black using a point or edge for a startling effect.
- Embark on a study of crayons, colors or shapes.

* Caution: Hot wax!

Invisible Ink

K-3   Caution

What could be better for a quick and simple secret message?

Materials:

citrus juice
white paper
writing instruments (paintbrush, cotton swab, toothpick, feather, pen nib)
small bowl
heat source (toaster, light bulb, hot radiator) (NEVER use an open flame!)

Process:

1. Squeeze juice from an orange, lemon or grapefruit into a small container.
2. Write a secret message on white paper using a writing instrument and juice.
3. Heat the note to reveal the message. When the message receiver wants to read this mysterious message, he must heat it up over a toaster or close to a light bulb with assistance. Stop heating as soon as the message appears.

Try This:

- Incorporate with a study of detectives, Halloween or mystery.
- Encourage interest in the written word with these invisible messages.
- Set up a Writing Center. What creative substances can the students think of to write with? Offer the juice as a medium for messages. Discuss the results of this effort. Have students guess what will happen when the message is heated. Investigate why this happens.

* Caution: Be careful when using heat source.

Paints

Children can roll up their sleeves and dig their hands into some slippery, colorful fun with finger paints or grab a brush and create masterpieces. Exploration with paints appears to have the added benefit of soothing kids and adults. Provide the opportunity to paint whenever you feel it is needed. Most powdered paints will wash out, but food coloring will stain, so have paint smocks available.

Safe "Oil" Paint

K-3

An earth friendly, kid safe, shiny alternative to oils. It responds like the paints of the masters.

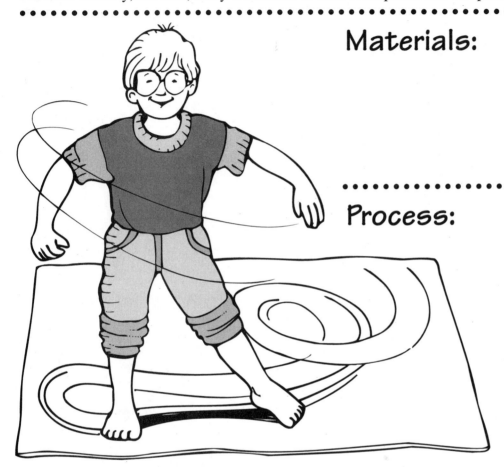

Materials:

small containers
stir sticks
natural pigment
vegetable oil

Process:

1. Put a little pigment in each container.
2. Add oil to each container and stir.
3. Add enough oil to give the texture you want for your project.
4. Allow projects to dry overnight.

Try This:

- Children can create interesting textures by adding unusual ingredients to any paint recipe–provide salt, coffee grounds, whole wheat flour, sand, vanilla, cinnamon, perfume, liquid soap, talcum powder, glitter, grain and rice for a start!
- Cover dark paper with a thick layer of paint. While the paint is wet, make designs through the paint with various objects.
- This thick paint works well for hand and foot paintings. Try a large mural.
- Try using sponges or rags to create interesting designs.
- Use this as a steppingstone for a study of art history.
- Discuss texture and the senses. Take students on a "texture hunt." Record their findings.
- Provide materials at a texture table where students can create substances of various textures.

Egg Tempera

K-3

Materials:

2 eggs
mixing bowl
water
spoon
containers
natural pigment
vegetable oil

Process:

1. Crack two raw eggs into a bowl. Separate the eggs and save the yolks.
2. Add a little bit of water and stir until you make a smooth, runny syrup. Pour it into several small containers.
3. Add pigment to each dish to create the colors you want.
4. Paint with your egg tempera paint on heavy paper or cloth.

Try This:

• Use nature to make interesting prints. Find leaves or flowers, press into the painting and remove. It will leave a print of the plant.
• Cut fruit or vegetables in half and make prints. Press the cut side into the paint and gently press onto paper and lift off.

Mud Paint

Materials:

mud
tray
sieve or sifter
bowl
blunt knife or craft stick
water
pigment
paper
paintbrushes
jars with lids

Process:

1. Gather the main ingredient–mud–from just about anywhere. (Use sterile potting soil if you are unsure about your outdoor sources.)
2. Strain the mud through a sieve or sifter.
3. Spread the strained mud on a tray to dry in the sun.
4. When dry, place in a bowl. Add a few drops of water and some pigment.
5. Mix with a craft stick or blunt knife until the mixture is paint-like. Add water to thin paint or dirt to thicken it. Kids will love to experiment.
6. Dip a paintbrush in and experiment with a new paint.
7. Store the dry paint indefinitely in jars with lids and labels.

Try This:

- Kids can finger paint with this stuff for a neat textural experience.
- Collection of the mud can be an adventure in itself.
- Tie this activity in with a geology study of rocks, the effect of wind and tides on rocks and a microscopic study of the grains of sand.
- Incorporate into a unit on science or geography.

Splatter Paint

K-3

A great new way to paint beautiful masterpieces of bursting color! Introduces kids to motor skills involved in squirting and spraying. Provides new forms to be described and observed.

Materials:

4 cups (1000 ml) flour
1 cup (250 ml) salt
1/2 cup (125 ml) sugar
powdered tempera paint
5 cups (1250 ml) water
bristol board or heavy paper

spoon
bowl
funnel
squirt top or large-hole spray
 bottles (liquid soap containers,
 glue bottles, plant sprayers)

Process:

1. Measure and mix dry ingredients in a bowl.
2. Add water and stir until there are no lumps.
3. Use a funnel to pour this mixture into a squirt bottle.
4. Cover the work area with newspaper and squirt, spray and splatter away! Heavy papers (including the kind you make) and bristol board work best.
5. Lay creations flat to dry.

Try This:

- Tip and wiggle creations before the paint dries for fascinating dribble pictures.
- Frame these masterpieces with a plain border to set them off effectively.
- Put your wet painting in a tray or box lid with some marbles. Tip and tilt to get the marbles rolling for an amazing effect.

Glitter Squeeze Paint

K-3

Materials:

1 cup (250 ml) flour
1 cup (250 ml) salt
1 cup (250 ml) water
food coloring
spoon
bowl
squeeze-top bottles
funnel
heavy paper or cardboard

Process:

1. Mix flour, salt and water together in bowl until well blended.
2. Add food coloring until you get the desired color.
3. Pour into squeeze bottles.
4. Squeeze onto heavy paper.
5. Let thoroughly dry for glittery effect.

Try This:

- Food coloring can stain. Students should wear painting smocks for this activity.
- Paint fireworks scenes on black construction paper.

Soapy Paint

K-3

Materials:

1/2 cup (125 ml) hot tap water
soap flakes to desired thickness
eggbeater
food coloring
pan

Process:

1. Pour 1/2 cup (125 ml) hot tap water in pan.
2. Add food coloring until you get the desired shade.
3. Mix with eggbeater until the paint has the consistency of whipped cream.
4. Paint away with fingers, feet or a large paintbrush.

Try This:

- Make a print. Place paper over the painting and gently press down. Remove to transfer the painting.
- Cover a painting with crumpled up cellophane wrap, foil, waxed paper, plastic bag, bubble wrap, foam egg carton or a string of beads. Allow to dry overnight. Remove carefully in the morning for an unusual texture.

Food Paint

 K-3

A mushy, satisfying experience!

Materials: yogurt, ketchup, whipped cream, oatmeal, cream of wheat, pudding, gelatin
large, plastic tablecloth
heavy paper or cardboard

Process:
1. Provide the medium and let children embark on a sensory experiment.
2. Create for creation's sake–don't try to keep these works of art!

Try This:
- Paint right on a table.
- Open up plastic garbage bags for a large plastic tablecloth.
- Experiment with adding pigments to these paints.

Puddle Paint

 K-3

Single servings of finger paint offer a rich tactile and visual experience.

Materials: ½ cup (125 ml) liquid starch
powdered or liquid tempera paint
heavy paper

Process:
1. Pour a puddle of liquid starch on paper.
2. Sprinkle a teaspoon of paint in the middle of the puddle.
3. Artistic fingers and hands do the mixing.

Try This:
- Freezer paper makes great inexpensive finger paint paper. Use the shiny side.
- Introduce new vocabulary–swirling, spreading, mixing, deepening, lightening and blending.
- Moisten the paper lightly with a damp sponge before using.
- Experiment with adding pigments to these paints.

Easy Finger Paints

Materials:

3 T (45 ml) sugar
1/2 cup (125 ml) cornstarch
2 cups (500 ml) cold water
food coloring
1/4 cup (60 ml) liquid
    washing detergent
4 cups
saucepan
spoon

Process:

1. Mix sugar and cornstarch together in the saucepan.
2. Add the water and stir as much as you like.
3. Put the saucepan over a burner on medium heat and stir constantly until the mixture comes to a boil.
4. Keep stirring until the paint mixture is thick and clear–about 6 minutes.
5. Remove from the element and cool for 5 to 15 minutes.
6. Pour the cool mixture into cups.
7. Add a little food coloring and a drop of detergent to each cup and stir until the paint is well blended.

Try This:

- Make a finger painting tray to keep the finger painter's work in place. Use the base of a cardboard box cut to have a 3/4" lip on all sides.
- Give students four small painting papers–have them number these. Play four musical selections (classical, children's pop, rhythm and blues and rock perhaps), and have students finger paint in the corresponding numbered paper to express the music.
- Set up a center with the various finger paints. Have students evaluate each one as they observe differences in texture and color. Follow up by graphing their conclusions.

Recycled Finger Paint

 K-3

Environmentally friendly smearing fun!

Materials:

1/2 cup (125 ml) discarded soap chips
1 cup (250 ml) cornstarch
6 cups (1500 ml) water
large saucepan
large mixing spoon
grinding stone

ladle
stir sticks
colored chalk ends or ground natural pigment
individual storage containers with lids and labels

Process:

1. Put chalk and soap chips in separate bags.
2. Break soap chips into fine pieces on the grinding stone.
3. Combine soap chips, cornstarch and water in the pan.
4. Bring the mixture to a boil over medium heat and stir constantly until the mixture thickens.
5. Remove the mixture from the heat and pour into individual containers.
6. When the mixture is warm, students can mix one color of crushed chalk to each container.
7. Let cool and store in covered, labelled containers.

Try This:

- Provide a table full of interesting items for students to experiment in the paint with: combs, toothbrushes, coins, balls, jacks, marbles, toy cars, feathers, rubber stamps, paper clips, elastics, rings, washers, sponges, sections of fruits and vegetables, leaves, flower petals and more. Just ask for suggestions!

Face Paint

K-3

This is just the thing when a class is ready for a new look!

Materials for Each Group:

8 tsp (40 ml) cornstarch
4 tsp (20 ml) water
4 tsp (20 ml) mild cold cream
food coloring
8-cup muffin tin
1 mirror
washcloths
mild soap

Process:

1. Split a class into groups for this activity. Provide one muffin tin per group.
2. In each cup of the muffin cup stir 1 teaspoon (5 ml) cornstarch, 1/2 teaspoon (2.5 ml) water, 1/2 teaspoon (2.5 ml) cold cream and 2 to 3 drops of food coloring–no more or the paint will be hard to remove. In the end there should be a different color in each cup.
3. The group members form partners, share the muffin tins and paint away.
4. Mirrors can enhance the facial artwork and encourage some dramatic play.
5. Students should wash up before going home. Supply some soft cloths and gentle soap.

Try This:

• Faces can be painted to complement a particular theme or dramatic presentation.
• Offer this activity with free exploration and experimentation. Try it again after viewing some examples and learning some face painting technique.
• The mixing in each cup of various quantities begs for a math lesson!

Foamy Fun Body Paint

 K-3   SPACE

An end-of-the-year-in-the-school-yard-with-a-sprinkler activity.

Materials:

bathing suits
towels
muffin tins

spoon
can of shaving or whipped cream
food coloring

Process:

1. Squirt the shaving cream into the muffin cups.
2. Add drops of various colors to each cup and mix with a spoon.
3. Change into bathing suits and meet at an outdoor location.
4. Use hands, sponges, cloths or paintbrushes to turn one another into works of art.
5. A few trips through the sprinkler, in the sprinkling skipping rope or under the hose will clean things right up.

Try This:

- Use several cans of shaving or whipped cream to create foamy multicolored sculptures.
- Have a Beard Day where students give each other creamy beards.
- Have students create costumes on one another to enhance a theme.

Camouflage Body Paint

K-3

Materials:

dusting powder of cool, white ash or fine earth particles
clay, mud or ground charcoal
cloths, towels and gentle soap for cleaning up

Process:

1. Wear camouflage clothing or old bathing suits.
2. Cover exposed areas with a thin dusting of crushed white ash.
3. Cover dusted areas with clay, mud or cool ground charcoal. (If clay is used, dusting is not necessary.)

Try This:

- Play games where children try to blend in with their surroundings.
- Have children turn themselves into critters and creatures of the forest with this activity.
- Use this activity to teach children about animal camouflage techniques and the necessity for this.
- Investigate various aboriginal peoples around the world who use camouflage techniques for their survival.

Chapter 3

To Model and Sculpt
Something to Sink Your Hands Into

There's nothing quite like digging your hands into soft gooey stuff and making something. Homemade play doughs and clays are simple to make, easy to work with, kind to the environment and you won't have to raid the school coffers to get them.

There are formulas for many types of modelling goo from soft, squishy and smelly to the kinds that harden up for works of art children can keep.

Play dough offers a medium for children to expand their abilities. It invites imaginative play, fine motor skill development, intellectual development, an early understanding of physics concepts, hand-eye coordination and social skills if group activities are undertaken. Play dough seems to have a soothing effect on students who spend time poking, flattening, rolling and squeezing.

Try out these neat doughs and clays to find the stuff you like to squish around with best. Students can experiment with ingredients and colors to invent their own formulas. They will find that the magic of creating these blobs is as much fun as using them.

There is a whole world waiting to get out of that blob of goo (easy, expressive)!

- -

Aims:

- To create a wide variety of molding media.
- To utilize a wide range of modelling media to express oneself in individual works of art.

- -

Objectives:

- Child will develop skill in manipulation of modelling and sculpting materials.
- Child will extend aesthetic sense through manipulation of modelling materials.

- -

Tips and Tricks:

- Educators should handle the alum powder. If you do not need to store your dough, this can be eliminated from recipes.
- If you want to keep your dough or clay soft for a time, store it in a recycled plastic container or plastic bag securely tied closed.
- If your play dough smells a little funny or is growing hair, it's time to toss it out.
- Play dough will keep longer in the fridge, but it will take a moment to warm up . . . hand heat works great!
- The only tools you really need are your hands. Shape coils, balls and cylinders. Flatten them into boxes, pancakes and ribbons. These basic shapes can be made in all sizes and variations to create almost anything you want.

TLC10009 Copyright © Teaching & Learning Company, Carthage, IL 62321

Make-in-a-Minute Dough

 K-3

This is the easiest play dough to make. It's fast and simple, and the ingredients are always on hand. It is very soft for little hands to work; it won't hurt a child who eats some by mistake!

Materials:

3 cups (750 ml) flour
1/2 cup (125 ml) salad oil

1/2 cup (125 ml) water
food coloring

Process:

1. Add food coloring to the water until the right shade is achieved.
2. Use spoons and hands to mix flour, oil and enough colored water to turn this messy blob into a ball.
3. Knead the ball well and it's ready to use.
4. Store in airtight containter.

Try This:

- Different colors allow for all kinds of possibilities. Make several colors at once. Create your own colors.
- Use diagrams to illustrate proper kneading technique.
- Allow kids to mess around with this dough without any instructions. Once they have explored all of their possibilities, you can sink your hands in and demonstrate rolling dough, rolling a "snake," making balls, marking using tools, poking with tools, shaping with cutters, folding . . . .
- Observe how a child manipulates the dough. Can the child pound, break up, stick to other surfaces, roll, flatten, pinch, squeeze, press, stroke, pat . . . ?

No-Cook Salt Dough

K-3

No fuss, no muss, no heat and this recipe lasts a long time.

Materials:

1 cup (250 ml) white flour
1/2 cup (125 ml) salt
3 T (45 ml) vegetable oil
1 tsp (5 ml) alum (available at drugstores)
1/2 cup (125 ml) water (may not all be needed)

Process:

1. Stir all ingredients together.
2. Add a little or a lot of food coloring to the water.
3. Add small amounts of colored water (about a spoonful at a time) until the mixture looks like play dough.
4. Store in an airtight container or plastic bag.

Try This:

- Encourage kids to mix colors to create ones you don't have.
- Offer the dough on its own so kids can explore only the dough.
- Offer interesting tools later to teach manipulation of instruments. Let children explore the tools without imposing preconceived notions of how they should be used.
- Create interesting shapes and designs with the following things found around the house–forks, knives, spoons and other utensils, toothbrushes, cloth, wood, shoe soles, toy blocks, cookie cutters, screwdrivers, soap holders, toothpicks, sharp pencils and thread.
- Press dough through a garlic press for neat hair, string, spaghetti, squiggles, worms.
- Observe to see if the child begins to name textures, shapes and tools.

Magic Lump

K-3

Turn a mess into the best fun around. This version lasts a long time.

Materials:

1 cup (250 ml) white flour
1/3 cup (80 ml) salt
2 tsp (10 ml) food coloring
1 T (15 ml) vegetable oil

2 T (30 ml) cream of tartar
1 cup (250 ml) water
plastic bag or airtight container

Process:

1. Mix all ingredients together in a saucepan over low-medium heat for about 5 minutes.
2. Stir until the mixture forms a lump in the middle of the pot.
3. Dump the hot blob onto a floured surface.
4. When the blob is cool enough–squish it, punch it and knead it.
5. Store in an airtight container in a cool place–preferably a refrigerator.

Try This:

- Discuss play dough with your class. What makes it great? What makes it a flop? Provide samples of the various doughs for students to rate.
- Diagrams and the written word can be combined for this survey. Compile the results on a pictograph for discussion.

Awesome Dough

This easy, long-lasting dough is a delight to play with.

Materials:

¹/₂ cup (125 ml) salt
1³/₄ cups (430 ml) water
food coloring or tempera powder
2 cups (500 ml) sifted all-purpose flour
2 T (30 ml) salad oil
2 T (30 ml) alum (available at drugstores)

Process:

1. Boil salt and water until the salt dissolves.

2. Add food coloring or tempera powder for color.

3. Stir in flour, salad oil and alum.

4. When cool enough, knead until the dough has an even consistency.

5. Keep in an airtight container or a plastic bag at room temperature.

Try This:

- Substitute cornmeal or whole wheat flour for the all-purpose flour to achieve an interesting consistency.
- Allow yourself a spacious workplace that won't be disturbed by an active child. Add to the creations to make scenes, villages . . . worlds!

Smelly Dough

 K-3

An experience for hands and noses!

Materials:

2 cups (500 ml) water
1/2 cup (125 ml) salt
1/2 cup (125 ml) flavored
  instant drink crystals
  (See options below.)
2 T (30 ml)
  pure vegetable oil
2 T (30 ml)
  powdered alum
2 cups (500 ml)
  all-purpose flour
food coloring (optional)

Process:

1. Stir water, salt and crystals, cocoa or extract (see choices) in a large pot over medium heat.
2. When mixture comes to a boil, remove it from heat.
3. Use a wooden spoon to stir in oil, alum, food coloring and flour.
4. Use your hands when the sticky mixture starts to form a ball.
5. When the ball is cool enough to handle, roll it onto a flat surface.
6. Knead until smooth.

Note: Modify the basic recipe to achieve the scent and color of dough you desire. See the choices below.

Try This:

Berry: Add at least 1/2 cup (125 ml) of berry-flavored crystals to desired strength of scent and color. A few drops of food coloring can be added for brighter color.

Chocolate: Dissolve 1/2 cup (125 ml) pure cocoa powder into hot water. Increase oil to 1/4 cup (60 ml).

Lemon: Add 2 tablespoons (30 ml) lemon extract. Add yellow food coloring until the desired shade is reached.

Peppermint: Add 2 tablespoons (30 ml) mint extract and green food coloring.

Bubble Gum: Add 2 tablespoons (30 ml) anise extract and red food coloring.

Soap Clay

K-3

. . . .

Materials:

1½ cup (375 ml) soap flakes
4 T (60 ml) hot tap water
food coloring (optional)

hand mixer
large bowl

. . . .

Process:

1. Add food coloring to water.

2. Mix soap and water in bowl.

3. Beat with mixer until the mixture has the consistency of thick dough.

4. Shape the clay into creations.

5. Let dry thoroughly–this creation can be admired or used as a soap.

. . . .

Try This:

- Leave the soap clay white for wintry works. Create an entire snow scene with the class creations. Begin with snowballs and expand on the "snowy" limits.
- Make a blob or block. Let it dry slightly. Carve a sculpture using a plastic knife.

Bounce and Stretch

K-3

Materials:

2 T (30 ml) white glue
4 T (60 ml) water
1/4 tsp borax powder
food coloring

2 cups
stir stick or tiny spoon
airtight container

Process:

1. Add coloring and 1 tablespoon (15 ml) of water to cup and stir.
2. Add glue and let sit.
3. In the other cup, add borax to 3 tablespoons (45 ml) of water. Stir until completely dissolved.
4. Stir the borax mixture constantly as you add the glue mixture.
5. Dump the rubbery blob onto a flat surface.
6. Knead until slippery and pliable.
7. Squish, squeeze, sculpt and bounce it!
8. Store in an airtight container for up to one week.

Try This:

- Stretch a ball of this dough over a colored comic or newsprint picture, press firmly and remove. This will pick up the picture which can be stretched into funny forms and faces.
- Play catch with a friend.
- An extra teaspoon of starch will make this more rubbery.
- You can work in a little water if this starts to dry out.

Creator's Clay

 K-3

For permanent works.

Materials:

4 cups (1000 ml) baking soda
1 cup (250 ml) cornstarch
1¼ cups (310 ml) cold water
saucepan
spoon
rolling pin
baking tray
cookie cutters
straw
sealer and/or paint
sealed container

Process:

1. Mix baking soda and cornstarch in saucepan.
2. Add water and cook over medium heat, stirring constantly.
3. When mixture is the consistency of moist mashed potatoes, dump it onto a plate.
4. Cover with a damp cloth until cool enough to handle.
5. Gently pat until it is a smooth ball.
6. Put in a sealed container for 24 hours before using.
7. Store in a sealed container in a refrigerator–bringing to room temperature before use.
8. Form shapes or roll to about ¼" (.6 cm) in thickness and cut with cookie cutters. If you want a hole, remember to do it while the dough is still soft. Use the straw.
9. Allow to air-dry or bake in a 200-250°F (93-121°C) oven for 2 to 3 hours until thoroughly dry.

Creator's Clay

K-3

Try This:

- Make decorations, jewelry, badges, buttons.
- Make marbles and then play with them in the school yard.
- Pasta, acorns, sand or other art materials may be added to create an interesting effect.
- Put a straw through your creation before it dries to make a hole for thread, string or ribbon to hang your piece as a necklace or decoration.
- Baked or dried pieces can be glued to beds, dressers, door frames, window frames, treasure boxes, with an adult's help and a glue gun.
- Most doughs can be frozen and defrosted. Bring the clay to room temperature before using, or it will be difficult to work with.

Cinnamon Clay

Materials:

1 cup (250 ml) cinnamon
1/4 cup (60 ml) white glue
1/4 to 1/2 cup (60 to 125 ml) water
ornament hooks or string
rolling pin
cookie cutters
straw
ribbon

Process:

1. Preheat oven to 200°F (93°C).
2. Mix all ingredients together in a large bowl.
3. Mix with hands until a nice soft ball forms.
4. Roll the ball on a flat surface using a rolling pin. Roll the clay until it is as thick as your finger.
5. Shape or cut with cookie cutters to make ornaments.
6. Poke a hole through each ornament with a straw or pencil.
7. Place the ornaments in a warm oven. Turn them every 5 to 10 minutes.
8. When they are firm, take them out to cool.
9. Place a ribbon through the hole and tie in a knot or bow so the creation can be hung somewhere for all to see.

Try This:

- Experiment with nutmeg, cloves and other spices.
- Almost any cylindrical object can be substituted for a rolling pin. Anything that rolls the dough out flat will do the trick. Incorporate a geometry lesson into a search for substitute rolling pins.

Bread-Rock Dough

 K-3

Bakes hard as a rock. Save your teeth; don't take a bite!

. . . .

Materials:

4 cups (1000 ml) all-purpose flour
1 cup (250 ml) salt
1½ cups (375 ml) cold water
2 T (30 ml) white liquid soap
paper clips

. . . .

Process:

1. Combine flour and salt in a large bowl.
2. Mix water and soap in a separate bowl; then pour over flour.
3. Stir quickly to combine.
4. Knead dough with hands until it is smooth.
5. Line a rimmed baking sheet with foil.
6. Shape handfuls of dough into creations. Tiny bread loaves, buns and creatures are only a beginning.
7. Bend paper clips around and press one end into dough to make hangers if desired.
8. Place creations on foil and bake in a 150°F (65°C) oven for 4 to 6 hours or until hard.

. . . .

Try This:

• When creations are thoroughly dry, paint with acrylic or water paints. When dry, apply a sealer so they will keep for years in a dry place.

Edible Sculpture Dough

K-3

No fuss, no muss, no heat and this recipe lasts a long time.

Materials:

1 packet dry yeast
1/2 cup (125 ml) warm water
1 egg
1/4 cup (60 ml) honey
1/4 cup (60 ml) sugar
1 tsp (5 ml) salt

1/4 cup (60 ml) margarine
1 cup (250 ml) milk
5 cups (1250 ml) flour
mixing bowl
spoon
cookie sheet

Process:

1. Mix half a cup of water with yeast until dissolved.
2. Separate the egg yolk and mix with sugar, honey, margarine and milk. Save the egg white for later.
3. Mix with yeast mixture.
4. Add salt and enough flour to make it firm.
5. Knead dough for 5 to 10 minutes and allow to rise for 1 hour.
6. Preheat oven to 350°F (177°C).
7. Form into shapes and sculptures and place on ungreased cookie sheet.
8. Whisk up egg white and paint it over top of the dough shapes.
9. Bake for 35 minutes in oven at 350°F (177°C).

Try This:

- Create theme-oriented breads and shapes.
- Make numbers, letters, even your name out of dough.
- Sculptures can be eaten or sealed for creations that will last for three months.

44

Sand Smush

K-3

Materials:

2 cups (500 ml) sand
1 cup (250 ml) cornstarch
1 T (15 ml) alum
3/4 cup (180 ml) water
old pot
wooden spoon
newspaper

Process:

1. Stir sand, cornstarch, alum and water in the old pot until well mixed.
2. Put the pot over low heat and stir constantly until the mixture thickens to look like dough.
3. Take the pot off of the heat and let it cool.
4. When the messy mixture cools, model it into sand creations.
5. Let the sand sculptures dry at room temperature. Drying time will vary according to size of creations–expect anywhere from two to five days.

Try This:

- When the masterpiece is completely dry, sand it very gently with fine sandpaper. This will remove loose grains and give the piece a smooth look.
- Your creation can be painted–painting with a small sponge will give the work a marbled effect.
- Seal the finished creation with a finish of white glue applied with a paintbrush. (Other sealants include glazes, clear enamel sprays, lacquers or nail polish.)
- Sculpt characters and scenes from a story being studied in the classroom.

Sand Clay

K-3

Materials:

6 cups (1500 ml) sand
1 cup (250 ml) white glue
water as needed
interesting containers
strong, flat surface for working
mixing bucket
stir stick

Process:

1. Mix glue and sand.

2. Add enough water to make it shapable.

3. Pack the mixture into containers.

4. Turn upside down and remove container.

5. Air-dry to harden.

Try This:

- For containers, try boxes, jelly molds, cans, cups, buckets, cardboard tubes, etc.
- Work as a group to create the best-lasting sand castle ever.
- Create an entire village with castles, trees, roads, animals, rivers, lakes, islands and more.
- Make flags on toothpicks ahead of time. Poke these into the sculpture before it dries.
- Make windows and doors by poking carefully with a tool of choice.
- When dry and hard, these creations can be painted.
- Are students able to problem solve to put the large shapes on the bottom of their structures?

Sawdust Dough

K-3

Materials:
2 cups (500 ml) sawdust
1 cup (250 ml) flour
2 tsp (10 ml) white glue

2 tsp (10 ml) starch
large bowl
large spoon

Process:
1. Mix the dry ingredients together.
2. Moisten with starch, glue and water to gain a good modelling consistency.
3. Model around a wire or stick frame. Pat modelling mixture onto the frame, shaping as desired.
4. Allow creations to harden for a permanent work of art.
5. Finish with a coat of shellac or paint.

Try This:

- Ask students to suggest other possible modelling materials.
- Incorporate with a geography unit. Have students create raised maps or land structures, such as mountains, islands, continents, etc.

Gathered Natural Clay

K-3

Materials:

clay deposit
sealed container for storing clay
bucket
smooth, hard surface
tools for digging
water

Materials for Tempering Agent:

grinding stone
any of seashells, pieces of brick, eggshells, old pottery

Process:

1. Research, inquire, ask local kids, gardeners or artists if they know of a good place to find a natural underground clay deposit. Kids enjoy seeking information regarding this form of "buried treasure." You might find a deposit at a building site, beneath grass and topsoil, but the best place to look is the banks of a creek. Get permission before digging!
2. Once you have found your clay deposit, gather it in a bucket with water.
3. Mush it and break up lumps with your fingers. Remove any impurities or debris.
4. Pour this "slip" mixture through a sieve.
5. Stir in a tempering agent. The clay should consist of 10 to 25% tempering agent. This will help prevent the clay from cracking, especially if the work is to be fired.
6. Let it stand for 12 hours.
7. Pour off the excess water.
8. Work the clay to get out air bubbles. Each student can repeatedly slam, pound, lift and turn the clay on a hard, smooth surface to remove any air bubbles and make it workable.
9. Shape the clay into sculptures, pots, bowls or other creations. Moisten or let the clay dry as needed to keep it pliable.
10. Keep unfinished pieces in plastic bags or sealed containers so they won't dry out.
11. Once you have shaped the clay into something you want to keep, let it dry thoroughly in a warm, breezy place with little temperature fluctuation and no moisture.

48

Gathered Natural Clay

Process for Tempering Agent:

Crush and grind the material to a fine talc.

Try This:

- Use the clay to make pots, bowls, plaques, pencil holders, chimes, beads, etc.
- Natural clay can be yellow, red, brown or grayish color–let students explore the properties of these different clays.
- Study pot shapes of early peoples. How did they evolve? What are the benefits of various shapes?
- Make pots using a leaf-lined hole in the ground to shape the pot and hold it as you work.
- Shape the bottom of your pot by forming the clay around a pot or container. Build from this base up using clay coils or snakes. Work the coils together gently. To widen the pot, place coils slightly on the outside of the previous layer. To make the pot narrower, place the coils slightly on the inside.
- When the pot is formed but wet, etch designs or use objects to make interesting textures.
- When the work has dried to a leathery texture, rub it carefully with a smooth surface to give it a polished finish.
- A dried piece of clay work is called greenware. Investigate the processes involved in creating a finished piece of pottery.
- For a hard permanent piece, you can fire work. To make greenware into permanent clay pieces, a process called firing must take place in a very hot oven or fire called a kiln. A local pottery or art studio might allow you to fire pieces there.

Pulpy Plaster

Materials: 4 cups (1000 ml) torn newsprint water

1 tsp (5 ml) white glue
1 cup (250 ml) plaster of Paris

Process:
1. Tear newsprint into small pieces.
2. Add water to torn newsprint until you have a soupy mixture.
3. Let pulpy mixture stand in a bowl overnight.
4. Mix in glue and plaster of Paris until the mixture has a modelling consistency.
5. Form into creative shapes and sculptures.
6. Let dry at room temperature.

Try This:
• Add lightweight decorative items to the surface of the plaster piece before it dries.
• Encourage aesthetic appreciation by showing slides or photographs of famous sculpted works.

* Caution: Don't breathe plaster dust!

Chapter 4
Stirrings to Stick With

Collages, creatures, construction paper towns, all need that most important craft supply–good old glue. It need not be fancy if it does the sticky job of holding things together on the paper, the sculpture or the fabulous creation of children's making. Students feel a sense of accomplishment at making this very basic craft supply. A little dab will do it with these easy glues that can be made in the classroom.

Aims:
- To create a wide variety of glues.
- To utilize a wide range of glues to allow expression of oneself in individual works of art.

Objectives:
- Child will assist in the making of a variety of glues.
- Child will develop skill in manipulation of glues, gluing tools and gluing techniques.
- Child will gain expertise in creating works by sticking objects together.
- Child will perceive and plan projects that will use a sticking substance.

Skill Development:
- Intellectual
- Emotional
- Language
- Social
- Fine Motor

Curriculum Links:
- Language
- Science
- Physical Education
- History
- Math
- Art
- Drama
- Geography

Tips and Tricks:
- It is a good idea to cover a work area when glue is involved. Although most glues wash up, it is much easier to just roll up the newspaper and be rid of the cleaning job. Some glues are worse than others.
- A smock or paint shirt will keep young artists glue-free.
- If you use your finger as a glue stick, before you know it your work will get sticky and muddled. Use a tool! A glue stick can be just about anything from a craft stick, a paintbrush, a stick or a cotton swab to a factory-made, bendable, plastic glue stick.
- Liquid starch makes a good paste for light papers.

Homemade Glue

....

Materials:

3/4 cup (180 ml) water
2 T (30 ml) corn syrup
1 tsp (5 ml) white vinegar

1/2 cup (125 ml) cornstarch
3/4 cup (180 ml) water

....

Process:

1. Bring 3/4 cup (180 ml) water, corn syrup and 1 teaspoon (5 ml) white vinegar to a full rolling boil.
2. In another bowl, mix together cornstarch and 3/4 cup cold water.
3. Slowly add the cornstarch mixture to the hot mixture, stirring constantly.
4. Let stand overnight before using.

....

Try This:

- Glue layers of tissue paper one on top of the other as each dries over various objects to form "stained glass" works of art. Plastic bottles and interesting boxes become treasures!
- Make a collage of a collection. Use glue to show off items.

Papier-Mâché Paste

K-3   SPACE

. . . .

Materials:

newspaper
1 cup (250 ml) flour
3 cups (750 ml) water
saucepan
wooden spoon

. . . .

Process:

1. Soak newspaper in bucket overnight. Squeeze out excess water.
2. Place flour in saucepan and gradually add water. Heat the mixture, stirring constantly to prevent lumps.
3. Boil for 5 minutes, stirring constantly until it thickens to a creamy consistency.
4. Let the mixture cool.
5. Tear paper (newsprint, newspaper, tissue paper or rice paper) into strips.
6. When the mixture is cool, the strips can be coated with it–by dipping and wiping.
7. Coat strips and mold around forms such as balloons, wooden frames, wire shapes, cardboard tubes, boxes or plastic bottles one layer at a time.
8. Let one layer dry completely (approximately 24 hours, depending upon the form), and then add another layer.
9. Add 6 or 7 layers to create a solid, interesting sculpture.

. . . .

Try This:

- Sculpt with paper by squeezing and building a design or shape.
- Make a piñata for a special occasion. Cover a balloon in layers of paper and paste. When all layers have dried, pop the balloon. (Don't worry if it breaks along the way, after the first layers have dried, it doesn't matter.) Fill a top hole with treasures and treats. Using a large needle, pull string through the top of the piñata so it can be hung. Let it dry until it is very light and hard. Hang it and allow friends to take turns batting it with a stick. It will break easily to spill the treats.
- Decorate your sculpture with paint, glue and glitter, tissue paper flowers, collages of stamps, magazine pictures, feathers or any neat thing that will stick to your creation.

Rice Paste

K-3

A nice paste for any paper.

Materials:

rice
heavy aluminum foil or
   plastic
hammer or rolling pin
storage container with a
   lid

saucepan with lid
stove
permanent marker
1¹/₂ cups (375 ml) water
strainer or colander

Process:

1. Place about ¹/₂ cup (125 ml) water and ¹/₂ cup (125 ml) rice into a container with a lid.
2. Cover and let the mixture stand for a week.
3. Drain off water.
4. Pour rice onto aluminum foil or heavy plastic wrap.
5. Crush rice with a hammer or rolling pin.
6. Pour crushed rice into saucepan with 1 cup (250 ml) of water.
7. Bring to a rolling boil, stirring constantly.
8. Reduce heat to simmer until mixture thickens.
9. Strain mixture with a colander or strainer over storage container.
10. Allow the liquid to cool and become the rice paste.
11. Store in airtight, labelled container.

Try This:

- For variety, add color to the paste and use for gluing collages of sand, grains or paper.

Easy Flour Paste

K-3

Can be used to paste any paper, but performs best as a papier-mâché glue.

. . . .

Materials:

1 cup (250 ml) flour   bowl
$^2/_3$ cup (160 ml) water   spoon

. . . .

Process:

1. Spoon a small amount of flour into bowl and add water.
2. Mix together flour and water until mixture is smooth.
3. Add more water if the mixture is too stiff or more flour if the mixture is too runny.

. . . .

Try This:

- Papier-mâché can be modelled like clay. Students can use it to make beads, dolls, masks and puppet heads.

Rawhide Glue

  1-3

Materials:

rawhide strips or rawhide dog bone
water (enough to cover rawhide in pot)
old cooking pot
stove

Process:

1. Put rawhide in cooking pot.

2. Add enough water to cover rawhide.

3. Boil gently until rawhide turns into thick mush. Time will vary, depending upon size of rawhide.

4. Let sit until mush cools and thickens.

5. You can boil further if you desire a thicker glue, or add water if you desire a thinner glue.

Try This:

• Only a small amount of this glue is needed. It works best on natural materials.
• Make wreaths using sticks, acorns, nuts, seeds and other objects.
• Create small stick scarecrow people using this glue to hold together sticks for the body and decorations to bring the scarecrow to life.
• Investigate how other glues are made.
• Cook in a well-ventilated area to minimize odor.

Crude Pitch Glue

2-3

Materials:

tree pitch
tree pitch hardening agent:
    cool white ash, ground
    eggshell or seashell
grinding stone
tongs
heat source

Process:

1. Gather pitch from an injured pine, spruce, fir, hemlock, cedar, yew, juniper or tamarack tree. Look for sticky dark substance semihard or dripping from the tree. Collect it on a stick.
2. Grind hardening agent: ashes, eggshell or seashells with a grinding stone.
3. Using tongs, hold the pitch piece over the area to be glued.
4. Apply a heat source such as a candle to the pitch and watch it drip onto the surface.
5. Sprinkle with hardening agent to make the glue magically harden before your eyes.

Try This:

- Learn about trees as you search for and gather the pitch. Use a tree identification guide. Encourage students to observe and discuss details about the trees.
- Use the pitch to make a stick "log house" for birds.

* Caution: Be careful when using a heat source.

Chapter 5

Dyes and Colors
Colors of the Rainbow

Interested in turning a collection of old shirts, socks or hats into a masterpiece of nature's colors? Until the mid 1800s all dyes came from natural materials. All the colors of the rainbow can be found in plant parts and transferred to materials with a little lesson in dyes. Natural dyes produce subtle colors and are less polluting than synthetic dyes. Have students explore the school yard for color sources. Put those dandelions to good use! Some dye sources can be bought at the market or found in the gardens of students.

Aims:
- To explore colors and means to transfer these colors to fabrics.
- To investigate plants as sources of color.

Objectives:
- Child will develop an appreciation for subtlety of color.
- Child will recognize various plants and their use as a dye source.
- Child will gain experience in a variety of dyeing processes.
- Child will become familiar with the terms and processes of transferring color to materials.
- Child will acquire skill in making and using dye baths which will give several colors to various materials.

Skill Development:
- Intellectual
- Emotional
- Language
- Social
- Fine Motor

Curriculum Links:
- Language
- Science
- Geography
- Health
- Math
- Art
- History
- Physical Education

Dye Source Color Chart

There are various field guides available to help with plant identification. Plants listed below are surprising sources of color. The colors given are an approximation of dye results. The more plant you use, the deeper the color will be.

. . . .

Plant	Part	Color
blue lupine	flowers	pale green
broom	flowers	peach
Celandine	flowers	yellow
crocus	flowers (purple)	blue-green
daffodil	petals	yellow
dahlias	flowers	burnt orange
dandelion	flowers	bright yellow
goldenrod	flower heads	yellow, beige, gold
heather	flower tips	green
marigold	flower heads	brass
Queen Anne's lace	flower and stalk	pale yellow
sunflower	flowers	soft yellow
tansy	flowers	yellow
wild rose	hips	oatmeal brown
yarrow	flowers	light green/yellow
zinnias	flowers	burnt orange
agrimony	leaves and stalk	peach
beet	leaves and roots	pinkish green
birch	leaves	beige
broccoli	stalks	green
cabbage (purple)	leaves	blue-lavender
carrot	tops	yellow
comfrey	leaves	yellow
elderberry	leaves	beige
grass	leaves	green
hyssop	leaves	dark green
lamb's quarters	leaves	yellow green
lily of the valley	leaves	spring green
mullein	leaves and stalk	green
parsley	leaves	light green
peach	leaves	beige
pear	leaves	beige
plum	leaves	beige
poplar	leaves	orange/gold
rhododendron	leaves	beige
smartweed	all but roots	yellow-green
spinach	leaves	green

Dye Source Color Chart

Plant	Part	Color
stinging nettle	all but roots	light brown
sumac	leaves	browns
tea	leaves	light brown, rose, tan
alkanet	roots	brown
beet	root	gold, pinkish/green (let stand 2 days in half vinegar, half water salt rinse)
bloodroot	roots	dusty rose
dandelion	root	blue/gray
water lily	root	brown
blackberries	berries	purple/blue
blueberries	berries	deep blue
cranberries	berries	red
elderberries	berries	lavender
juniper mistletoe	berries	purple/gray
purple grape	fruit	wine
raspberries	berries	burgundy
rose hips	berries	red/pink
wild holly	berries	pale pink
apple	inner bark	light brown no mordant
birch	inner bark	light brown no mordant
hemlock	inner bark	light brown no mordant
oak	inner bark	brown no mordant
walnut	inner bark	light brown no mordant
black walnut	shells	dark brown no mordant
bracken fern	curled head	yellow green
coffee	beans	yellow tan
fenugreek	seeds	yellow brown
lichens		soft beiges and browns to pinks (soak in vinegar)
red onion	skins	mirky green
red clay	surface water	red
yellow onion	skins	light brown, burnt orange, yellow

60

Natural Dyes

Many natural materials from the yard or garden can be used to create subtle dyes.

Materials:

dye source material (see list)
large cooking pot (stainless steel glass or enamel) with lid
8 cups (2000 ml) soft water
stove
storage containers with lids
wooden spoon
colander or strainer
large mixing bowl
cotton string, natural wool or a
    cotton T-shirt
rubber gloves (to protect from heat and staining)
apron (to protect clothing)
Mordant (for 1 lb of material)
4 ounces (113 g) alum
2 T (30 ml) cream of tartar
4 gallons (15.12 l) soft or distilled water

Process:

1. Gather roots, berries, barks, flowers, leaves and plants in the following seasons:
   flowers: when young and vigorous, gather into a container of water. Handle gently.
   leaves: when first out in full (spring)
   berries: when slightly over ripe
   bark: spring from prunings or a felled tree
   roots: late summer and fall
   lichens: in damp weather
2. Break the plant pieces into small bits.
3. Combine the water and plant pieces in the pot. Do not use less than 1 cup (250 ml) of dye source material for a pint (.47 l) of water. More dye source material will make a stronger dye (1 gallon [3.78 l] boiling water/4 ounces [113 g] material to be dyed). Measure out the dye source material and water for the color you desire. Let the dye stuff soak in cold water for: bark–7 days; berries–1 to 2 days; flowers–1¹/₂ hours; leaves and stalks–2 days; roots–4 days; spices, coffee and tea–no more than 1 hour.

* Caution: Work in a well-ventilated area–outdoors. Do not ingest dyes or mordant, as some of these may be toxic. Wash hands after handling materials or use rubber gloves as some materials are irritants.

Natural Dyes

Process:

4. Bring to a boil.
5. Strain the dyestuff material and resume boiling the liquid.
6. Cover dyestuff mixture with lid and bring to a boil. Continue boiling gently for about 1 hour, until water turns the color you desire. Stir occasionally.
7. Only a few natural dyes have good fastness to light and washing. Most require a mordant to fix the dye to the fabric. If the item is to stand up to washing, see Mordant below. Soak the items you plan to dye in fresh water or mordant–squeeze out excess water.
8. Add your items to the dye bath pot and simmer gently until desired color is achieved–about 1 hour. Wet fabric will look darker than it will once it has dried.
9. Remove pot from heat, leave items in dye bath to cool.
10. When cool, remove items from the pot, squeeze out excess water and hang or lay flat to dry.

Materials for 1 lb (40 kg) Mordant:

4 ounces (113 g) alum
2 T (30 ml) cream of tartar
4 gallons (15.12 l) soft or distilled water

Process for Mordant:

1. Add ingredients to the water in saucepan, stir and gently boil material for 15 minutes.
2. Add material and simmer gently for 1 hour.
3. Let material stand in liquid until cool.
4. Remove the item and squeeze out excess moisture. Dye the damp article or let dry and dye at another time.
   (A mordant can alter the color of the dye.)

* Caution: Work in a well-ventilated area–outdoors. Do not ingest dyes or mordant, as some of these may be toxic. Wash hands after handling materials or use rubber gloves as some materials are irritants.

Natural Dyes

K-3

Try This:

- Enhance observation skills through a scavenger hunt for dye sources.
- Encourage students to experiment to find other colors.
- Have students guess and record what color they think each source will produce.
- Try tie-dye! Bind, pleat, fold, knot, twist, scrunch, crumple and tie with thin string before putting material in dye bath. Try wrapping buttons, marbles or other small shapes and tie tightly. Try dipping corners only. Let dry before untying.
- Try batik! Melt a wax of 1/2 paraffin and beeswax. Paint a design on the fabric using wax and a paintbrush, toothpick, eyedropper or a cotton swab. Immerse in cold water. Add to the dye bath. Creates very interesting patterns! (For a simpler and safer but less effective method, draw on fabric with crayon, then dip in dye for a batik effect.)
- Incorporate with a study of plants. Consult an identification guide to help you find the right plant, flower, fruit or vegetable.
- Incorporate with a unit on native and pioneer peoples who used nature's colors to color the cotton, wool and linen fabrics they wore.
- Make a game of matching the dye source with cloth dyed by that source. Design a bulletin board to display the dye source and the cloth dyed by it.

Neat Things to Dye:

T-shirts	cloth swatches
canvas shoes	shorts
paper	pants
napkins	kite string
bathing suits	socks
towels	hats
school bags	gloves
marble bags	pillowcases
tissue paper	hair ribbons
feathers	bookmarks
eggs	

* Caution: Work in a well-ventilated area–outdoors. Do not ingest dyes or mordant, as some of these may be toxic. Wash hands after handling materials or use rubber gloves as some materials are irritants.

Kool Dyes

Materials:

2 packages of unsweetened
   powdered drink mix
stainless steel, glass or enamel
   cooking pot with lid
1/2 cup (125 ml) white vinegar
1/2 gallon (1.89 l) water

stove
storage containers with lids for
   dyes (glass jars, plastic
   containers)
items to be dyed

Process:

1. Pour two packages of unsweetened Kool-Aid™ or powdered drink mix
   into cooking pot.
2. Add vinegar and water.
3. Cover and heat until pot steams.
4. Simmer for 20 to 30 minutes.
5. Let cool and pour dyes into storage containers or dye bath.
6. Soak item to be dyed in pot of dye until desired shade is reached.

Try This:

- Paint dye on fabric with brush or cotton swab.
- Dye napkins, place mats, bookmarks or paper for a school fund-raising activity.
- Purchase some indigo or madder dye at supply shops–these produce lovely colors.
- Incorporate a lesson on measurement and time, as needed for the recipe.
- Use pictographs to record students favorite colors.

64

Golden Eggs

2-3

A traditional European onion skin dying method. Each egg will be different.

Materials:

cold water
12 or more onions, dark
    skins only
12 raw white eggs
small elastic bands
muslin
large pot
stove

Process:

1. Remove onion skins and soak for 5 minutes in a large pot filled with cold water.
2. Drain the skins into a colander.
3. Wrap 2 or 3 layers of skin around raw egg. Wrap in muslin. Fasten skins with elastic bands. A tie-dyed effect will appear where the elastic bands are fastened.
4. Layer eggs in pot.
5. Completely cover eggs with cold water.
6. Bring water to a boil over medium-high heat.
7. Reduce heat and simmer eggs for 10 minutes, partially covered.
8. Remove pot from heat.
9. Remove the egg and plunge into cold water.
10. Remove the muslin and onion skins.
11. Dry carefully. Refrigerate until needed in empty egg carton.

Try This:

- Rub with cooking oil for a shiny appearance.
- Use eggs for a centerpiece in a basket.
- Add other colors to egg with felt pens or attach transfers.
- Draw with white crayon on egg before dyeing for a batik effect.
- Hard-boil egg before dyeing to help prevent breakage.
- Experiment with a variety of natural materials to achieve a variety of colors.

Resources
Evaluating a Child's Creative Progress

••

How does an educator evaluate a child's progress in a K-3 art program? Observe the individual child in a wide variety of art experiences. Focus on the child's growth and the process of creating rather than the end products. An exciting learning environment should facilitate the development of fine motor skills, language abilities, imaginative play, and social and emotional skills. A broad base of concepts and skills should be achieved during the various developmental stages.

••

Child three to five years of age will:

- participate with natural enthusiasm and spontaneity
- express himself freely
- manipulate materials in creative ways
- make use of found materials
- use language throughout an activity
- use tools in a manner limited by fine motor skill development
- use materials with a purpose
- become visually aware of details
- experiment with texture, form and color
- demonstrate a sustained interest in an art activity

••

Child five to seven years of age will:

- participate with natural enthusiasm and spontaneity
- express himself freely
- manipulate materials in creative ways
- make use of found materials
- use language throughout an activity
- recognize similarities and differences
- develop visual awareness of fine detail, scale, design, conservation, symmetry and color
- produce symbolic forms for a variety of familiar objects
- combine forms to express ideas, feelings or to tell a story
- demonstrate changes in intellectual growth through drawings
- combine materials in inventive ways
- demonstrate a variety of problem-solving techniques
- develop and use a growing art vocabulary
- participate in group efforts
- demonstrate a sustained interest in an art activity
- become self-motivated

Resources

Evaluating a Child's Creative Progress

. . . .

Child seven to nine years of age will:

- participate with natural enthusiasm and spontaneity
- express himself freely
- manipulate materials in creative ways
- make use of found materials
- make use of advanced language before, during and after engaging in artistic activity
- manipulate tools and materials in a competent manner
- combine forms to express an idea
- make use of a rich art vocabulary
- demonstrate an increasing understanding of perspective, scale, proportion, profile, balance, design, horizontal and vertical lines, space, fine detail, design, color, texture, mood and motion
- develop a need for finer tools
- pre-plan works through discussion and sketches
- use art to communicate ideas
- integrate art skills with other subjects
- work well with others on projects
- demonstrate a sustained interest in an art activity

Evaluation of the Child

You may wish to use this checklist several times per child during the year. Date your evaluation so you can compare and note areas of progress.

Child's name _____ Does the child . . .	Never	Some-times	Always
Make use of found materials?			
Use material with a purpose?			
Use art to communicate ideas?			
Experiment and manipulate materials freely in various media?			
Explore all the qualities of the media provided?			
Solve problems in an inventive manner?			
Produce a wide variety of symbolic forms?			
Use vocabulary that indicates artistic knowledge?			
Show attention to detail, color, texture, mood and motion?			
Demonstrate a working knowledge of the tools needed to create in the medium?			
Demonstrate the ability to organize and plan a project?			
Make use of a variety of techniques to create and complete works?			
Organize and present artwork in a creative way?			
Demonstrate initiative in art tasks?			
Work well in group projects?			
Incorporate independent thinking and problem-solving skills when creating a work?			
Demonstrate a degree of visual awareness appropriate to his or her age level?			
Demonstrate an increasing awareness of composition and detail?			
Make use of an understanding of arrangement, perspective, balance, scale, proportion, profile, conservation, symmetry, size of objects and use of space?			
Express ideas about the work verbally?			
Offer comments that demonstrate insight into various experiences?			
Complete given projects?			
Demonstrate progressive skill development?			
Demonstrate increasing appreciation of aesthetics?			
Show an appreciation of classmates' efforts and differences?			
Consolidate art skills with other subjects?			
Appraise his own work?			
Take pride in her work?			
Demonstrate a sustained interest and joy in artistic activity?			

Evaluation of the Artwork

Does the artwork demonstrate . . .

- originality?
- expression of personal feeling?
- good use of the media provided?
- an understanding of the skills needed?
- pride in work?
- a sense of harmony?

Cumulative art portfolios provide an excellent record of a child's progress and provide a base for discussion and evaluation.

Everything has its beauty but not everyone sees it.
Confucius

Evaluation of the Program

A sound art program should encourage creativity, stimulate language, develop aesthetic skills, enable plenty of experimentation, act as a vehicle for self-expression, reinforce a positive self-concept, aid in the development of physical coordination and lead to a feeling of joy.

Does the program . . .

- allow for individual creative expression?
- provide opportunities to manipulate and explore various media?
- offer developmental lessons with general direction and purpose?
- allow for the sequential development of the relevant art skills associated with the program?
- reinforce a child's positive self-concept?
- provide experiences which bring joy to the participation?

Scavenger Lists

Where Can I Find Free Materials?

• •

Search, discover and recover! Prepare a letter to send home with students that lists the kind of materials your classroom could use. Let them know you collect "good" junk. Save packaging of all kinds. Enlist the help of local businesses, most have at least a little trash that could be put to good use in your classroom. Send out a letter stating your interest in their excess materials. Some businesses will even donate small samples of perfectly good stuff!

Check out your local resources with the eye of a scavenger! Here are a few suggestions:

interior decorator's business	wall covering store
floor covering store	upholstery store
hardware store	appliance store
graphic arts studio	framing shop
art supply store	print shop
local newspaper office	bookstore
computer shop	electronic component shop
school recycling bin	recycling center
orthodontist's office	doctor's office
lumberyard	woodworking shop
building site	auto repair shop
fast food restaurant	cafeteria
grocery store	food market
dry cleaning store	laundromat
moving company	airline company
floral shop	garden center
feed supply store	local farm
garage sale	thrift shop
attics	junk drawer
craft bins	basements

• •

Try This:

• Provide shopkeepers and business owners with a large box that has your name on it, and ask them to save interesting scraps for you. Pick up your box once a month.

Materials Worth Scavenging

computer paper
wallpaper sample books
shredded paper
paper bags
frame shop mat scraps
old posters
used envelopes
used stamps
newspapers
magazines
cardboard
paper rolls
paper cups
junk mail
boxes
milk cartons
Styrofoam™ packing peanuts
Styrofoam™ trays
bubble wrap
foam balls
tin trays and pans
tinfoil
straws
stir sticks
craft sticks
rubber bands
carpet and flooring scraps
fabric scraps
quilter's scraps
thread
fabric samples
old clothing
buttons
odd socks
thread spools
shoelaces
string
yarn
twine

waxed floss
bows
ribbon
jar seals
pipe cleaners
marker lids
crayon stubs
candle stubs
beeswax
balloons
old hoses
puzzle pieces
plasticine
hardware
wood scraps
old paint
plastic bags
coat hangers
plastic tubs and containers
jars
crates
computer disks
computer chips
discarded computer equipment
electronic components
broken clocks
broken kitchen appliances
old telephones
discarded toys
old jewelry
old beads
fruit baskets
food containers
old signs
keys
flowers
straw
pennies
carpet and flooring scraps

Bibliography

Bakule, Paula Dreifus, Ed., *Rodale's Book of Practical Formulas; Easy-to-Make, Easy-to-Use Recipes for Hundreds of Everyday Activities and Tasks*. U.S. Rodale Press, Inc., 1991.

Brown, Rachel. *The Weaving, Spinning and Dying Book*, 2nd Edition. Alfred A. Knopf, New York, 1983.

Burt, Erica. Illustrated by Malcolm S. Walker. *Natural Materials*. Bourke Enterprises, Inc., Vero Beach, FL, 1990.

Charles, Oz. *How Is a Crayon Made?* Simon & Schuster, New York, 1988.

Drake, Jane, and Ann Love. Illustrated by Heather Collins. *The Kids Cottage Book*. Kids Can Press. U.S. Distribution, Tricknor and Fields, 1993.

Erickson, Donna. Illustrated by David LaRochelle. *Prime Time Together . . . with Kids*. Discovery Toys, Augsburg Fortress, Minneapolis, 1989.

Fiarotta, Phyliss. *Snips and Snails and Walnut Whales*. Workman Publishing Co., 1975.

Graham, Ada. *Foxtails, Ferns and Fish Scales: A Handbook of Art and Nature Projects*. Four Winds Press, 1976.

Kohl, Mary Ann F. Illustrated by Kathleen Kerr. *Mudworks, Creative Clay, Dough and Modeling Experiences: Bright Ideas for Learning Centers*. Bellingham, WA, 1989.

Kohl, Mary Ann R. *Scribble Cookies and Other Independent Creative Art Experiences for Children: Bright Ideas for Learning Centers*. Bellingham, WA, 1989.

MacKay, Sharon, and David MacLeod. Illustrated by Marilyn Mets. *Chalk Around the Block*. Somerville House Publishing, Toronto, 1993.

Norris, Doreen, and Joyce Boucher. *Observing Children in the Formative Years*. The Board of Education for the city of Toronto, Toronto, 1980.

Palmer, John. *Drawing and Sketching*. Ron Ranson's Painting School Series. Anaya Publishers Ltd., Strode House, London, 1993.